Anne Wilde Talks Modern-day Polygamy

Copyright © 2017

Gospel Tangents

All Rights Reserved

Except for book reviews, no content may be reproduced without written permission.

2nd Edition

Table of Contents

Introduction

Gospel Tangents needs your support. Please consider donating to our website, https://GospelTangents.com in any amount. We will use your donation, and the information from these podcasts to produce professional Mormon History Documentaries and other resources such as this.

Anne Wilde knows modern day Mormon polygamy better than almost anyone. She was the second wife of Ogden Kraut, helping him write 65 books on LDS Church history and doctrine, and is the co-founder of *Principle Voices*, a group founded to support polygamy in the United States. Anne knows Mormon polygamy groups like the Apostolic United Brethren, FLDS, Centennial Park, the Kingston and Harmston groups, and her husband even had a close encounter with Ervil LeBaron, a polygamist responsible for the death of at least 20 people. Anne gives a glimpse into these groups, and details her own marriage. She talks about the theological basis for polygamy, and even believes Jesus was a polygamist. For an inside look into Mormon schismatic groups, check out this transcript of our 2 hour interview! We'll answer these and many other questions.

(Note this conversation was recorded on June 21, 2017 in Salt Lake City, Utah. I will use GT for Gospel Tangents to indicate when I am talking to Anne. I'd like to thank Anne for reviewing the transcript and emending it for improved readability, clarity, and accuracy. Revisions are noted with square brackets [] and/or footnotes.)

Taylor's Un-canonized 1886 Polygamy Revelation

Introduction

Is it true that President John Taylor had a revelation in 1886 proclaiming
that polygamy is an eternal principle? Polygamist Mormons think so.
I'd like to introduce Anne Wilde. She's a fundamentalist Mormon
polygamist herself, and is one of the biggest experts on modern-day
polygamy that I know of. I'm really excited to talk to her. We'll ask her
about the split between the mainstream LDS Church and polygamists in
this day. We'll also ask her if she thinks the current LDS Church is in
apostasy. Check out our conversation…..

The Interview

GT: Welcome to *Gospel Tangents Podcast*. I'm here with Anne Wilde.
Anne is an independent fundamentalist Mormon and I would say is
probably one of the biggest experts on polygamy, modern-day
polygamy, that I know at least. Is there anybody else that knows more
than you? {Chuckles}

Anne: It's just because I'm so old. I've been around and
experienced a lot of it for many years.

GT: Well great. Anyway, this has been funny. I recently interviewed
Brian Hales about his books on Joseph Smith's polygamy.[1] I interviewed
a member of the Remnant Church of Jesus Christ of Latter-day Saints,
and he believes Joseph was a monogamist[2], and now you. We're
definitely talking a lot about polygamy lately.

Anne: Covering the bases, huh?

---

[1] Part 1 of 11 is available at https://gospeltangents.com/2017/06/09/canadian-
polygamy-should-it-be-legal/

[2] Part 8 of 9 with Jim Vun Cannon, counselor in First Presidency of Remnant
Church is found at https://wp.me/p8l6gx-hq

GT chuckles: Yes. We're getting a lot of different perspectives. That's what I'm trying to do here.

What I wanted to start talking about is how the rift occurred between I'll call it [early] Mormonism and the [mainstream] saints in Salt Lake. We kind of know that there was a split back in 1860 with the RLDS Church, and so I'd like to get into when the split occurred with the more modern fundamentalist polygamists. I was wondering if you could give us a little bit of history on how that started. I don't know if dispute is the right term with John Taylor. Is that a good place to start, or should we start before that?

Anne: Well I guess that's probably a good beginning—in 1886 when John Taylor claimed, and I personally believe, he received a revelation from the Lord regarding polygamy because at that time it was very controversial. [Government officials were] very much involved. They were coming out here and arresting polygamists.

[John Taylor] was approached about signing a manifesto of some sort in 1886 in order to get the government off our back so to speak. In the process he received this revelation. It's only one page, relatively short. But it said in there that the Lord would not change an eternal principle or an everlasting covenant. [Taylor] said that after he received that, he felt like he could not sign any kind of a compromise. He said that he would rather have his arm cut off or his tongue torn out rather than sign any kind of a compromise regarding doing away with plural marriage.

I guess it kind of started then, but when they issued the Manifesto in 1890,[3] that was a key part of the whole

---

[3] In 1890, church president Wilford Woodruff issued "The Manifesto" declaring that he advised Mormons not to contract in any more polygamous marriages. This is canonized as Official Declaration 1 in the Doctrine and Covenants. See

history. 1904 was the Second Manifesto, with Joseph F. Smith, that put a few more teeth in doing away with it. Then of course in the 1930s, Heber J. Grant issued what we call the Third Manifesto. That was kind of the final straw as far as polygamists were concerned because if they were found out to be living it then they were excommunicated from the church.

With each succeeding Manifesto, the teeth got a little stronger against us. In the 1930s you have the Lorin Woolley story where he felt like he should continue plural marriage. He called a group of seven men including himself that were commissioned to keep plural marriage alive, which he did. Gradually one by one they began dying off. There was Lorin Woolley, then Joseph Broadbent who was president of that council or senior member for only about six months, then John Y. Barlow, then Joseph Musser, and then there were three others after that.[4]

During the period of time of Joseph Musser, a lot of the men (and some of the women for a short time) ended up going to jail; they were arrested for plural marriage or cohabitation. [In 1944, 15 men were imprisoned, and after several months], they disagreed on whether or not they should sign a compromise or any kind of a document in order to get out of prison to go back to their families. Eleven of them ended up signing, and four of them did not. [This was the beginning of disunity among some of the polygamists. But that's] a whole other story in itself.

GT: Ok, let's back up a little bit. I want to go back to 1886 because you said some people were pressuring John Taylor, president of the church

---

https://www.lds.org/scriptures/dc-testament/od/1

[4] The others are (in order) are Charles Zitting, LeGrande Woolley, and Louis Kelsch.

at the time about issuing a manifesto. Who were some of these people? Were they government officials or LDS officials?

Anne: I think some of them were leaders of the church. I couldn't say names without going back through history, but I know that the [polygamists] were very leery about being arrested and being separated from their families. So they thought if John Taylor were to sign something, it would help them not have that fear and run the risk of being arrested for having more than one wife.

But when he refused to do that, I think he was really speaking for the priesthood of the church. But he was also speaking for the church, too, because as president, he spoke for the church. By not signing anything, that left the people who didn't want to live it high and dry, so to speak, because they were also at risk then of being arrested.

GT: Ok so I've heard, and I don't know how true this is, so you can tell me if this is a true story or not. I have heard that some people did not want Wilford Woodruff to be the next prophet because they were concerned that he would sign the Manifesto, or a similar one that John Taylor refused. Have you heard that story before?

Anne: I really haven't. I don't think when Wilford Woodruff became president of the church, he had in mind that he was going to sign a manifesto. I hadn't heard that. John Taylor died in 1887.

GT: This was about a year before [his death that] he received this revelation?

Anne: Yeah, right.

GT: Do you think he entertained doing a manifesto prior to [the] 1886, revelation?

Anne: [John Taylor] was president of the church for 10 years—five of those years at least he was in hiding. It was for plural marriage because he had more than one wife, and he continued taking them by the way.

GT: Even while he was in hiding?

Anne: Yes he did.

GT: Oh.

Anne: Let's see, back to your story—I have never heard that Wilford Woodruff was intending to sign a manifesto before he became president of the church. If that's a story you've heard, I'm not aware of it.

GT: Well it's not that I heard it...

Anne interrupts: [Woodruff] even prayed about it after he became president. What course should he take? He was shown in a dream or told there were two courses. He could sign a manifesto and get the government off their back, or the way it was worded, he could let the Lord fight their battles. Well, he chose what he thought was the best course for the church itself. So he decided to issue the Manifesto.

It's pretty hard to see a lot of the stalwart members of the church, priesthood bearers and so forth, end up behind bars. They were having a tough time financially. [Their settlement in] the valley was only about 40 years old. They were still trying to make a living and provide for [their families of sometimes] three or four wives. To have the major breadwinner in jail, that was pretty hard on the family and on the economy of the church. I can understand that.

A lot of fundamentalist Mormons are very critical of Wilford Woodruff for signing that Manifesto. In my personal understanding of it, I feel like he did what he thought was best for the church, but I think he knew that it was still a priesthood law, and that it could be lived by those that wanted to continue living it as a priesthood law, but they would risk their membership in the church by so doing. I'm not as critical of Wilford Woodruff and his signing that as maybe some people are. I really feel like he was doing what he thought was best for the members of the church, because by far, most of them didn't want to live it. Why should you enforce something that the majority of your followers don't even want to live? It's common sense to say you're trying to do what the majority wants.

GT: That's interesting. As far as this revelation, it seems like in the LDS Church, some people have disputed the authenticity of it. How do we know that's an authentic revelation?

Anne: Because there's a copy of it in John Taylor's handwriting. That's the main authenticity I can show. I have a photocopy of that in his handwriting. And it fits. [It's important to me that historical events "fit," and if they don't, I just put them] on a shelf for a while. To me the whole historical background of the 1886 fits, because somewhere there needed to be something to instill a desire and be the motivating factor for people to keep on living it. Without that, it would have been much more difficult, confusing. The Lord had made his voice very clear on [the subject of plural marriage in D & C Section 132[5] and] previously. I think He needed to reiterate that to give the saints the motivation and the courage to continue with it.

---

[5] See https://www.lds.org/scriptures/dc-testament/dc/132

GT: Ok so it's in his handwriting. I don't believe that revelation is public, or is it?

Anne: Oh anybody can find it by looking it up.

GT: It's online?

Anne: I don't know if it's online. I would imagine it is. I have a copy of it right here.

GT: Ok, I might have to get a copy of that. I'll have to post that with the interview.

Anne: It's very easily available—has been printed in books. I was one of Ogden Kraut's wives, and he included it in some of his books, and it's also in some of Brian Hales' books—an actual copy of the original. There is all kinds of evidence for it.

GT: Ok. I just talked with Curt Bench as well. You used to work and still kind of work with him.

Anne: [Occasionally, but I've officially retired.]

GT: You're emeritus I guess, right?

Anne: Yeah, that's a good way of putting it.

GT: I just saw you at one of the signings of the Mountain Meadows Massacre.[6] That's where we arranged this interview. The thought, especially [after talking] with Curt Bench, comes into my mind—is this a Hofmann forgery?[7] {Chuckles} How long has that been known about publicly? I would assume it dates well before Mark Hofmann.

---

[6] Richard Turley, Janiece Johnson, and LaJean Carruth have put together a documentary history of the trials of John D. Lee and many documents related to the Mountain Meadows Massacre. See http://amzn.to/2yLYfh6

[7] Part 1 of 7 of my interviews with Curt Bench can be found at https://gospeltangents.com/2017/05/19/bombs-in-salt-lake-introduction-to-mark-hofmann/

Anne: Oh absolutely. Ogden started writing books in 1969 and we knew about it before then. I think anybody that really wanted to find it could find it. Since a lot of fundamentalist Mormon history goes back to that important revelation, [we have known about it for decades.]

GT: Ok, so is that in LDS Church Archives, or where is it?

Anne: I'm sure it's up there somewhere. It might not be real easy to obtain because the church doesn't like to come out and make a big deal of it, but fundamentalist Mormons make a very big deal of it.

{break}

GT: As I understand it, John Taylor back in 1886 or so was concerned that the church may one day get rid of polygamy, so he ordained a small subset of men …

Anne: [Yes, a Priesthood Council (sometimes referred to as the Council of Friends)] that I mentioned before—men that were commissioned to keep plural marriage alive.

GT: Ok, so these men were supposed to keep it alive, even outside of the church if necessary, is that correct?

Anne: Well, I don't know if that was made specifically clear, [about it being done] even if it was outside the church. They were just commissioned to keep it alive, to see that not a year passed that a child was not born in plural marriage. At that time they didn't (I don't think) anticipate a manifesto in 1890. They probably thought that the church was eventually going to have to compromise in some way because the pressure was getting so strong from the government. So this was an avenue they could do it separate from the church, like I mentioned before as a priesthood law.

The thing is with plural marriage, it was a priesthood law to begin with. When Joseph Smith reinstituted it as a doctrine that came from the Old Testament originally, it was not a law of the church. He lived it secretly for many years. He appointed others to live it. It was not a law of the church until 1852 when they came out here to the [Salt Lake] Valley and Brigham Young brought it up.

So it was a law of the priesthood, then it became a law of the church in 1852 until 1890. Then it was no longer a law of the church but it was still a law of the priesthood. It was never _not_ a law of the priesthood.

GT: That's interesting.

Anne: That's how it has continued.

GT: Is it true that fundamentalist polygamist Mormons believe that essentially now we're living—excuse me not we, because I'm certainly not a polygamist, that's for sure; {Anne chuckles} that the fundamentalist polygamists are living in the same mode from—I don't know when you date the beginnings of polygamy, up to 1852?

Anne: It's similar, yeah. I guess regarding whether it's a law of the church or a law of the priesthood, that part is similar.

GT: Ok. We just had a discussion about this, an online discussion. I know Brian Hales brought up the point that if you're not part of the church, we don't recognize that priesthood.

Anne: I know. That's the stand of the church today.

GT: Right.

Anne: If you are not a member of the LDS Church, you
do not have that priesthood. I disagree with that because
the priesthood existed before the church was organized.
I mean they got the Aaronic Priesthood before 1830 so it
can exist, and has existed separate from the LDS Church.
[I believe that the] only way a man can lose priesthood is
not through excommunication from the church, [but
rather because of their own] sin. That's the way a man
can lose the priesthood.

If he has had it conferred correctly to begin with, and he
has not done anything that the Lord would not honor,
then he can still hold the priesthood outside the church.
The church is a vehicle through which the priesthood can
function. But if the church takes a course other than
supporting and obeying the eternal principles that the
priesthood is supposed to uphold, then which path do you
take? That's the decision we've had to make. Are we
going to abide by the eternal, unchangeable principles of
the gospel and the priesthood, or are we going to go
along with the church that has changed literally every
doctrine and ordinance of the gospel in some way? That's
the choice.

GT: Ok, I guess that brings up another question then. Do you consider
the current LDS Church in apostasy?

Anne: The D&C says that the Lord God will "set in order
the house of God." It has to be out of order before it can
be set in order. So, yes, I think to some [degree it is out
of order. Fundamentalists may disagree as] to what level
it needs to be set in order, but I think the time will come,
when as the Lord said, he "will send one mighty and
strong ... to set in order the ... house of God,"[8] house

---

[8] Anne seems to be referring to D&C 85:7. See

meaning kingdom. The church is part of the kingdom.
Yes, I do believe that things will reach a point where
things will have to be set in order.

Did Woodruff Marry After the 1890 Manifesto?

Introduction

In 1890 Wilford Woodruff issued what's known as the Manifesto, Official Declaration One[9] in the *Doctrine & Covenants*, prohibiting polygamy. What many Mormons don't know is that polygamy did not end in 1890. In fact, Wilford Woodruff himself may have married another wife in 1897, a year after statehood in Utah. We're going to talk in this episode about post-Manifesto polygamy. What are some of the things that led to the Second Manifesto in 1904? Anne Wilde, a polygamy expert will tell us why. Check out the conversation…..

The Interview

GT: Let's move on to post-Manifesto polygamy. There are some critics of the LDS Church that say the reason why Wilford Woodruff issued the Manifesto was he wanted statehood and he wanted to get the government off their backs, but he was still secretly practicing polygamy. It seems like there were some polygamist marriages going on. I know the judge, when that came out, was going to take it for what it said and it seemed like the LDS Church was stopping polygamy at least publicly. It does seem like it did move underground. Do you have any comments on whether you think that 1890 Manifesto was meant for public consumption, but privately we were still going to practice it, or how does that work?

Anne: I don't know what was in the back of Wilford Woodruff's mind. I don't know, but there's pretty good evidence that he himself took a plural wife seven years after the Manifesto. We also have very good evidence that many of the apostles, the Quorum of the Twelve, took additional wives after 1890. That's one reason why

---

[9] See https://www.lds.org/scriptures/dc-testament/od/1

the 1904 Manifesto had to come out is to put teeth in it because so many people were very quietly taking additional wives, especially in Canada and Mexico.

They were being sent there by some leaders of the church with a coded message to men like Anthony W. Ivins, or whoever was in Mexico or Canada that was designated to perform plural marriages outside of the United States. They had this note authorizing that it was ok with the leaders that they perform this plural marriage for the couple that presented the note. Very definitely there were very many plural marriages after 1890.

One of the best things that's ever been written on that period of time is Michael Quinn's *Post-Manifesto Polygamy*. It was in the 1985 *Dialogue* magazine, an article about 95 pages. It's absolutely amazing. [Michael] is so meticulous about footnotes, and he had all of these references and sources on people who took plural wives after 1890—many of whom were leaders of the church.

GT: Do we have any idea how many leaders of the church did take plural wives between 1890 and 1904?

Anne: Leaders of the church, that could include stake presidents and bishops, but among the Quorum of the Twelve, I think it was about half took additional wives.

GT: Ok.

Anne: I'd have to research that to be sure.

GT: Would you say that Wilford Woodruff didn't really mean the Manifesto if he was still taking plural wives?

Anne: He did it for the church. It was a press release really. Orson Pratt announced it in the fall [General] Conference of 1890. When the LDS Church issued the press release in late September, the U.S. government officials wouldn't accept it because it hadn't been voted on by the church. So the next conference, which was early October, they presented it for people to vote on.

I'll never forget the quote about B.H. Roberts who was sitting on the stand when they called for the vote [to accept the Manifesto.] He said, "It was the awfulest moment of my life. I could not vote for it, and did not."

GT: Oh really?

Anne: There were several experiences like that that other people had. Some of them were so happy they cheered. Others had tears in their eyes. A lot of them had questions, such as, "What do I do with my wives?"

It was a very tough time. I'm not going to judge Wilford Woodruff or anybody. I just would like to give them the benefit of the doubt.

GT: Ok.

Anne: It was a test. For those who really wanted to live it, there was still a way, but you couldn't live it with the consent of the church anymore.

GT: Well you could.

Anne: You could, but after 1904 you couldn't.

GT: Ok, so let's talk about 1904. What were the events going on in the church that led to the Second Manifesto?

Anne: The very fact that a lot of people had been taking additional wives. Joseph F. Smith himself had several wives. I think he just realized that the pressure was coming again from the government. [They accused the

Church of not meaning what they said. They figured out that there were still plural marriages being performed.

President Smith felt that something had to be done to reinstate or reinforce that decision of 1890, so he issued the Second Manifesto. This one stated that anyone who solemnized or entered into a plural marriage would be excommunicated from the LDS Church.]

GT: Did the 1890 Manifesto [apply to only those plural marriage performed] inside the United States?

Anne: Well it didn't say that specifically, but that's the way it was interpreted. [Since President Woodruff was speaking for the Church to the U.S. Government, the people responded,] "Oh well that only applies to the United States." He didn't say that in the Manifesto, but they interpreted it that [way because the Manifesto itself referred to U.S. Congress laws.] That's why they thought, "We can still [perform plural marriages] out of the country. We're not doing anything wrong."

GT: Is it true that people went to Mexico to obtain a plural sealing?

Anne: A lot of them took their prospective plural wives and went down to Mexico or Canada because there was somebody there designated to perform plural marriages.

GT: I've heard that Mitt Romney has some [ancestors who had more than one wife.]

Anne: Yeah, Miles [Park Romney (son of Miles Romney) was Mitt's great-grandfather, and he lived with his five wives] in Mexico.

GT: Ok. Miles Park Romney--did he actually live in Mexico?

Anne: Yes, as far as I understand.

GT: Ok, so he just went down there to get married and came back?

Anne: [No, he was living there to avoid arrest in Arizona. Sometimes plural families moved to Mexico to get away from the government.[10]]

GT: Ok, that's interesting. It seems to me that there was also another big issue in the early 1900s that may have led to the Second Manifesto and that was the Reed Smoot hearings.

Anne: Oh, right, in 1904.

GT: Can you talk about that?

Anne: What particularly? There are four big volumes about the Reed Smoot hearings. They didn't want to seat him, even though he had only one wife.

GT: From what I understand, he had been elected as a senator in Utah. Was that in 1900? I don't remember when it was.[11]

Anne: [1902. The hearing began in] 1904.[12]

GT: Ok. It seems as I recall, the history I remember is that the Senate did not want to seat Senator Smoot, and apostle Smoot, even though he was a monogamist because there was concern that Mormons were still doing polygamist marriages in the temples, against the 1890 Manifesto.

---

[10] According to Wikipedia, Miles Park Romney went to Mexico in April 1885 and lived there until his death Feb 26, 1904, in Colonia Dublin, Mexico. See https://en.wikipedia.org/wiki/Miles_Park_Romney (retrieved Oct 26, 2017).

[11] Reed Smoot was elected senator from Utah in 1902. He served in the U.S. Senate from 1903-1933. More info can be found at https://en.wikipedia.org/wiki/Reed_Smoot#United_States_Senate

[12] The hearings began in 1904 and continued until 1907, when the Senate voted. The vote fell short of a two-thirds majority needed to expel a member so he retained his seat. More info at https://en.wikipedia.org/wiki/Reed_Smoot_hearings

Anne: That's my understanding.

GT: Ok. That's probably what led the government to apply a little bit more pressure.

Anne: It was one of the reasons, I'm sure.

GT: It led Joseph F. Smith to issue the Second Manifesto.

Anne: Right, yeah.

GT: So that's what led to that. Now even with the 1904 Manifesto, as I recall, wasn't there an apostle or two that was excommunicated?

Anne: Yes there were two of them, John W. Taylor and Matthias Cowley. They were kind of scapegoats. The church felt that they had to do something to show the government they were serious about discontinuing plural marriage. So Matthias Cowley was disfellowshipped and John W. Taylor was excommunicated. Matthias Cowley was eventually reinstated.

GT: To the quorum or just to the church?

Anne: Just to the church; he was never put back into the quorum.

GT: Yeah I don't think so either.

Anne: Both of them were polygamists. I feel like the other members of the quorum decided that something had to be done to show the government that they were serious.

GT: Ok, so they were scapegoats. Now as I understand it, you were actually a member of the LDS Church for a number of years.

Anne: Many years. I was born and raised in it. I was excommunicated (I'm not going to say the date), but I was excommunicated because I had been a plural wife.

GT: Ok, I know I've heard another interview with you, and you said that many fundamentalist Mormons believe that the church is, even if it's in apostasy, it's still a good thing....

Anne: Absolutely.

GT: ...and that it does contain a lot of the important ordinances of the gospel. Is that true?

Anne: Well they've been changed to some degree, but it's still got a lot of good things about it. I'm glad that I was raised in it. I went to BYU, I loved going to school there. I still love the church. It does a lot of good. I even go [to LDS meetings] once in a while because I have friends there.

This is the way the Lord wants it. It's been all the way through history, this is what has happened. The Lord restores the gospel. It lasts like in the time of the Nephites for nearly 200 years, and then the people start making changes and fall away. It's nothing that hasn't been done in history before.

It doesn't get me all riled up where I can't sleep at night because of the changes that have been made. I feel like it's the way it's supposed to be. This is a test of people who really want to continue with these eternal principles. Plural marriage is just one of them. Then when things are set in order then the Lord will know which ones he can depend on to keep those principles alive.

GT: Ok, I believe, and tell me if I'm wrong here. Fundamentalists generally do like that LDS members go through the temple and they complete those ordinances. They recognize those ordinances and that priesthood. Is that true?

Anne: No.

GT: Oh that's not true.

Anne: There's a lot of fundamentalists that question whether or not the church still has priesthood authority. I don't know if we want to go into that for various reasons. I don't think there are many fundamentalists that think that the [LDS] temple work being done today is authentic or of any validity. Some fundamentalist groups have temples of their own where they do their own endowment work because they feel like they have the priesthood so it is of more efficacy than what the church is doing.

I think that's why we have a thousand years of the millennium to straighten all this out. I'm not going to say that the temple work being done today is authentic or not. That's up to the Lord to decide on that. But certainly temple work should be done with correct priesthood [authority to be recognized by God.]

Third Manifesto Causes Schism: Apostolic United Brethren

Introduction

So far we've talked about the 1890 Manifesto, as well as the 1904 Manifesto. A third manifesto was issued in 1933, and that actually led to the formation of several polygamist groups. In this next episode, we'll talk about the Third Manifesto, as well as one specific group: the Apostolic United Brethren. You may be familiar with them if you've watched the tv show, *Sister Wives*, with Kody Brown and his four wives. Check out our conversation with Anne Wilde.....

The Interview

GT: Let's jump back. We started going through the history and we'll jump back there again. We talked about up to 1890, then 1904. Then this period from 1904 to 1930ish.

Anne: 1933, I think.

GT: After the 1904 Manifesto was really the first time that a person could get excommunicated for practicing polygamy.

Anne: Yeah.

GT: I guess there were a lot of polygamists, so apparently they didn't excommunicate everybody immediately. but they said if you contracted a new marriage, that was grounds for excommunication.

Anne: Yes but some of them still did it in quiet. Let me just say that I know of cases without naming anybody [where a man took new wives and they remained] members of the church (in the last 20 years), but they were very quiet about it.

GT: So church leaders didn't know about it.

Anne: Yeah, and to be consistent, if they do find out, they will hold a court and they will be excommunicated, which is as it should be. It's right there in the [bishop's] handbook.

GT: So you're saying that this is still happening today. There are LDS members who are joining polygamy and still maintaining membership in the church.

Anne: Well, not a whole bunch of them.

GT: Not publicly.

Anne: Yeah, certainly not publicly, and not in great numbers; but there are isolated cases where that may be true.

GT: Ok. Let's talk about this period, you were talking about 1904-1933 and Joseph Musser. What was happening in that period between 1904 and 1933 and Joseph Musser?

Anne: You mean in the church? There weren't any groups until later on.

It's kind of like when the sun goes down, when does it get dark? It's just gradually. The term "fundamentalism" wasn't even used until probably in the 1950s. [LDS apostle] Mark E. Peterson and [polygamist] Joseph Musser both used that term about the same time. [There] was just not a real distinction of "here's a polygamist group over here and they believe in polygamy, and the church doesn't." It was just kind of they both went parallel together, with some people continuing it and the church gradually giving it up. When Joseph Musser became the senior member of the [Priesthood council]...

GT: … this quorum of seven?

Anne: Yes. There was this quorum of five in 1886, then [at least] two more were added.

GT interrupts: Is that what it's called, this quorum of five, this priesthood quorum?

Anne: Some people call it the Council of Friends or the Priesthood Council. It's called by different names, depending on who's telling the story.

GT interrupts: It doesn't have a specific name, I guess.

Anne: [Lorin Woolley was the last one alive from that 1886 Priesthood Council that John Taylor called. He] was told to call some other men to keep that principle alive, so he called another council.

GT: So he was one of the original [council, and the others] had died?

Anne: Yes, you had George Q. Cannon[13] [was added a short time later,] and Joseph F. Smith was called when he got back from his mission in the Sandwich Islands[14] as part of that council to keep polygamy [alive.] But this was all below the radar. So anyway, when they began dying off, then Lorin Woolley was the last one of that original council.

GT: Had they called people in to replace the ones who had already died, or he was it?

Anne: No, [he was it.]

GT: So they were down to one.

---

[13] In order of seniority there were John Taylor, John Woolley, Samuel Bateman, Charles Wilcken, and Lorin Woolley, George Q. Cannon and Joseph F. Smith.
[14] The Sandwich Islands are now known as the Hawaiian Islands.

Anne: Yes, down to one. [Lorin called these other men I've mentioned--Joseph Broadbent, John Y. Barlow, Joseph W. Musser, Legrande Woolley, Charles Zitting, and Louis Kelsch—but not all at once.] Anyway, when Joseph Musser was the senior member, because the other three before him had passed away, then that's when the "split" happened. It's too complicated to go into. Suffice it to say that there were two [men (LeRoy Johnson and Marion Hammon) that had been suggested as additions to that quorum, but Joseph Musser was not in favor. So, instead, he called Rulon Allred, Owen Allred, Marvin Allred and a few others to another council— so now we have two councils.]

GT: Two parallel councils.

Anne: Yes, and each one claims that they're the only ones that have the authority, or the true priesthood or whatever you want to call it. So that's when the division began. Joseph Musser died in 1954, so this happened before that.[15] {snip}

GT: 1933, why is that a pivotal year?

Anne: That's when Heber J. Grant [issued the third manifesto that really put the teeth in the church's stand against polygamy.]

GT: That was the third Manifesto.

Anne: There was a real division then, a real separation because there were some people that definitely felt [that they were supposed to continue living plural marriage because they knew it was an eternal principle. In 1886. God had said, "I have not revoked this law nor will I for it

---

[15] John Y. Barlow was head of the quorum until his death in December 1949.

is everlasting, and those who will enter into my glory must obey the conditions thereof." Using that and other things as a basis, several fundamentalists went on living the principle] separate from the church.

GT: Musser, up until 1933, was he a still a member of the LDS Church?

Anne: I'm not sure when he was actually excommunicated.[16]

GT: Ok.

Anne: There's a journal [and several books written about him. And Brian Hales] would probably know the year. I can't remember offhand. I do know he died in 1954.

GT: You said there were originally some apostles that were part of this council of five.

Anne: Yes, George Q. Cannon and Joseph F. Smith, [who were added later.]

GT: Ok, Joseph F. Smith. He's the one who issued the Second Manifesto.

Anne: Yes, it's ironic, isn't it?

GT: Wow.

Anne: But the pressure was so strong from the government. It's kind of like Wilford Woodruff. There was a lot of pressure, not only from the government but from the people inside the church. [Most church members] didn't want to live it. They didn't think the

---

[16] Musser was excommunicated in 1921. See https://web.archive.org/web/20131226181825/http://mormonfundamentalism.com/ChartLinks/JosephWhiteMusser.htm

church should [practice] it. It was giving [the Mormons] a bad name.

The majority of the people in 1890 didn't want to live it. They were glad when the Manifesto [was announced.] I think it was similar in 1904 when Joseph F. Smith felt pressure to [issue] another manifesto.

GT: In 1933 we got the Third Manifesto, and that's when the church was like, "We mean business."

Anne: Yes, and what's interesting is Heber J. Grant had three wives, and he made the statement that he was going to keep on living with them until somebody gave him a son—which never happened.

Yet there was a lot of [duplicity going on—saying one thing publicly and another thing privately. You can understand that. It was the same way in Joseph Smith's time. He'd say one thing publicly and do another privately. Not only was the world [unprepared] for what he was teaching, but [there were] a lot of converts from England, and polygamy was not a popular [teaching] with them. That's why [Joseph Smith] had to keep it quiet and [mention it] to only those men that were loyal to him and would accept it.

GT: So the idea is in 1933 you could not contract any new wives. You could keep living with the ones you already had.

Anne: I even think at that time it was recommended [that polygamist men could keep their youngest wives,] the ones they could still have children with. I don't think it was a hard and fast law and you could still recognize them as [wives, but you were not supposed to conceive children] with them; so that's why it was recommended you keep your youngest wife [so children could still be born in the family.]

GT: Ok, so in 1933 it sounds like there was a split among the polygamist groups. You've got the Allred group and the Musser group?

Anne: Well no, it wasn't [really called the Musser group at that time, because he called Rulon Allred to another council and his followers later became known as the Allred group. The senior member of the other group with headquarters in Short Creek was Leroy Johnson, and gradually they promoted what has been termed the "one man rule."]

GT: Ok, so the Allred group, if I am correct, is known as the AUB, the Apostolic United Brethren.

Anne: [Yes, that is correct.]

GT: Can you talk about the AUB group? What are some of their characteristics? I think most people are familiar with FLDS, but not as many people with the AUB.

Anne: The AUB has a priesthood council. The number varies from time to time. They have a senior member of that priesthood council. He's called the president of the priesthood in that group. They do not have the strict appointment and control over marriages that [the FLDS leader has] by any means. There's a lot more free agency.

[More than one council member] has the keys of sealing; the head of the group and then others that he designates can also perform marriage sealings. Their headquarters are in Bluffdale, [Utah] but they have communities in Montana, Mexico, Central Utah—little communities around. They have a membership of about 7,500. They have most of the same traditions [and organizational structure] as the LDS Church. For example, they have a Relief Society and priesthood meetings and things like that.

GT: Ok, you talked about a council. That wouldn't be like a Council of Twelve Apostles or anything?

Anne: Like I said, the number of the council varies.

GT: Ok, would they be analogous to a Quorum of Twelve?

Anne: Yes, kind of.

GT: But it doesn't necessarily have to be that.

Anne: As far as I know, they don't have a [First Presidency—a president and two counselors. I'm not a member of that group so I can't tell you for sure, but I have several friends that attend their meetings. We don't discuss a lot of what goes on in their group and I don't pry. But I know they have a president of the priesthood or a senior member of the council, one that is designated to be the leader, and then they have a number of apostles who are members of their priesthood council.]

GT: Ok, but they are like apostles?

Anne: I guess, yes, but I really can't speak for them.

GT: Yeah, ok. Is it true that Kody Brown, is he one of those?

Anne: Yeah, he came from that group and I think he still considers himself a member.

GT: Ok, I have to tell you. I think it's a little bit of a guilty pleasure that I love that show. It's not on Netflix so I haven't watched for a while.

Anne: [There are only so many episodes in each season, and then they take several months off to do the filming for the next season.]

GT: I know he lived in Lehi, Utah for a time. Last I remember, and I haven't watched the show in years, they moved to Las Vegas. I don't know if there's a big community in Las Vegas.

Anne: No.

GT: I wouldn't think so. In that case is he just doing kind of a home church sort of a thing?

Anne: Yes, they have their own family meetings on Sunday, and I think if he comes up here to Salt Lake to visit, he [probably] attends some of the meetings but I'm not sure. He doesn't come up that often, but now that [some of] his kids are going to school in [Utah] and getting married and so forth, he has reason to come back to Utah to visit [more often.]

GT: Ok, I know his daughter, I want to say Madison, I can't remember, was going to Utah State I believe and she actually wanted to join the LDS Church.

Anne: And they wouldn't let her.[17]

GT: And they wouldn't let her, and she said, "I don't want to be a polygamist. I don't want to do anything." But they still wouldn't let her. Essentially the church policy is that they want you to basically disown your parents, or I don't know if that's the right terminology.

Anne: I think that varies. Without mentioning a name, there is a [polygamous] family whose son joined the LDS Church, had friends that were [Mormons, and] went on a

---

[17] For more info, see http://kutv.com/news/entertainment/sister-wives-daughter-says-lds-church-wont-let-her-get-baptized

mission for the Church. He didn't have to deny his parents, but he had to deny his intent to live [plural marriage.] He now is back home after serving an honorable mission. He was not prevented from joining the church, even though [the authorities] knew what family he came from. So that's why I say, it's going to vary.

That was [Kody's daughter's experience, and I think it might have been because the Brown family had been so public and were so well known nationally, and if it got out that one of the daughters joined the LDS Church, maybe the leaders thought that it wouldn't look very good.]

GT: Yeah, ok. What do you think of that policy?

Anne: It seems to me that somebody is being punished for somebody else's transgression. I think there's an Article of Faith along those lines.[18]

GT: Yeah, I think so.

Anne: I think it's too bad if she sincerely, and I think she did, wanted to join the church, I certainly think she should have had that privilege. I call it a privilege because she looked at it that way.

---

[18] The 2nd Article of Faith states "We believe men are punished for their own sins and not for Adam's transgression." See https://www.lds.org/scriptures/pgp/a-of-f/1?lang=eng

How Do Polygamists Feel About Gay Marriage?

Introduction

Fundamentalist Mormons are known for promoting an alternative marriage practice in polygamy. Of course there are gay marriage advocates who support that as well. In this next episode, we'll talk a little bit about Kody Brown's oldest daughter, Mariah. Kody is a polygamist in the tv show, *Sister Wives*, and he has four wives. One of his oldest daughters has actually announced that she is gay. What do fundamentalist Mormons think about gay relationships? I hope you'll check out our conversation with Anne Wilde…..

The Interview

GT: I'm sure there are as many opinions as there are fundamentalists…

Anne: You're just about right.

GT chuckles: It seems like if I remember the show ["Sister Wives" correctly,] they did talk a little bit about gay marriage in one of the episodes.

Anne: One of the daughters is gay.

GT: This is before that. The one episode that I remember was they were talking about whether gay marriage should be legal, and as I recall Kody Brown was sitting around with his wives and they were like, "Yes consenting adults should be allowed to do whatever they want. It should be legal." I suspect, and we'll talk about the FLDS Church here in a minute, some of the other groups would find that policy heretical.

Anne: I cannot speak for a group as a whole, but the fundamentalists I know, don't have any problem with legal gay marriage [as a civil right.] That's not a religious sealing. That's a personal choice, and if we expect to have the country look at our [plural marriages as our civil right, and at least have them decriminalized], then we have to be willing to grant others their free agency in forming a family and [deciding who they marry. This is a big issue with us.]

The [fundamentalists] that I associate with don't think there's anything wrong with a legal gay marriage, because like I say it's not a religious [issue.] They think [that gays] should have that legal right. We're talking about a civil rights issue. They should have their civil rights just like we [should have ours.]

Now we feel like we already have the consent of the Lord because this is his ordinance, His marriage style and He's already indicated [that celestial plural marriage is] an eternal principle—so religiously, we feel like we already have the right to live plural marriage, but [unfortunately] we don't have the civil right, which seems backwards to me. So I feel like both gays and polygamists should have the civil right [and free agency to choose their marriage partners.]

GT: Ok.

Anne: What is ironic is that people used to tell us years ago, if the gays get their right to [legally marry, then it would be a slippery slope for polygamists to obtain the same legal right.] Well you know how that turned around? In the December 2013 Waddoups decision, [Judge Waddoups decriminalized plural marriage. We polygamists were very excited. A week after that, the Supreme Court gave gays the legal right to get a legal marriage license. But, really] ours came first.

GT : Now let's talk about that. You're talking about this Waddoups case. This was here in Utah...

Anne: That was in Utah,

GT: ...or was that a federal law?

Anne: ...and it was [later appealed by the [Utah] Attorney General, Sean Reyes. It took a while for the appeal to go to the Denver 10th Circuit Court, and then it took even longer for them to decide—they eventually overturned Waddoups' decision! So it's right back to where it was. In the state of Utah, cohabitation is not only illegal, it's a felony. It's one of the only states in the United States where it is a felony. They might call it cohabitation or polygamy or whatever they want, but it's still considered against the law.] If we are arrested and taken to court, we can be charged with a felony in Utah.

GT: I know Mark Shurtleff, and he's not the Attorney General anymore, he basically had the policy that if you're not breaking any other laws, he was going to look the other way. Sean Reyes is the new Attorney General. Does he have a similar policy?

Anne: Yes, I think basically he does, but he still couldn't let that [2013 decision stand.] I can't second guess Mark Shurtleff, but I [doubt that] he would have appealed it. [He knew several consenting-adult polygamists and had heard our side of the issue. He had held meetings with us in order to better understand our lifestyle. Sean Reyes] has not done that.

I think [Sean thought that this was necessary to save the] reputation of the Attorney General's office. He couldn't allow that [decision to stand without an appeal.]

GT: Ok, so in federal court it was basically re-criminalized...

Anne: Well, it was a district court in Denver that upheld the appeal.

GT: That's a federal court though, right?

Anne: It's a federal district court.

GT: Federal district court, ok. So has that been appealed to the Supreme Court or anything?

Anne: [Jonathan Turley, our attorney in the case,] did appeal it to the Supreme Court, but they refused to hear it because they didn't think there was enough evidence to make a change from the 10th Circuit Court's decision. So in other words, by refusing to hear it, that meant they upheld the district court's decision.

GT: So essentially the Utah law is now unchanged.

Anne: Right. In 1935 [polygamy was made a felony in the state of Utah, and that's the way it stands today.]

GT: It's a state law, and the state law has been upheld.

Anne: Really what was upheld was the [Utah] bigamy statute which has two prongs to it. It has the cohabitation prong and the purporting to be married [prong.] Well, we don't really run around purporting to be married [to more than one wife, and we get only one legal marriage license—so we don't feel like we're disobeying the purporting to be married prong. So there's no problem with keeping that part of the bigamy statute intact.]

But the cohabitation [prong was removed from the statute] by Waddoups because there are a lot of people that cohabit that aren't married. So if you were really going to enforce that, you'd have a lot of trouble finding all the cohabiting people [in the state. So we felt that Waddoups' decision, in essence, decriminalized plural marriage--which it did.

However, this can get really complicated. We have still got the 1935 felony state law on the books regarding polygamy, and we've also got our state constitution declaring that polygamy shall forever be prohibited. So it is problematical as to how the Waddoups' decision could have been compatible with these two? It's confusing.]

GT: Well, let's jump back to the [gay] issue. The LDS Church in November 2015 issued a [policy] statement in the handbook that said the Church was] not going to baptize children of gay parents any more.

Anne: Until they are 18.

GT: Until they are 18. One of the things that they cited was, this is how we've always treated polygamist [children] so therefore how we [will be treating] children of gays is consistent. What do you think of that policy?

Anne: I was very disappointed in that decision for many reasons. I'll just give you one example. I worked at an [LDS] bookstore [for several years.] The day after that decision was [announced, a customer] came into the bookstore and said, "There's a young girl, eight years old, in our ward. She is living in a home with gay parents and she is scheduled to be baptized Saturday. [Because of this decision,] they will not let her be baptized." [That breaks my heart. Friends in her Primary and Sunday School classes will all be baptized at age eight. How do you explain to her that she can't be baptized, too?

That's just one of many situations that came up. I just felt bad about it. You're punishing children for what I don't even think is a civil sin of the parents. The parents wanted her to be a member of the LDS Church. They wanted her to go to Primary. They [personally took her to church every Sunday.]

GT: I think I remember reading about that in the paper. There's probably more than one.

Anne: So anyway, that was just one of many [sad situations resulting from the church's decision.]

FLDS-Centennial Park Rivalry

Introduction

We're continuing our conversation with Anne Wilde. She's a modern-day polygamy expert. In this next conversation we'll talk about the FLDS Church. Many of you are probably familiar with the FLDS group and their prophet Warren Jeffs who is currently serving time in a Texas prison. We'll also talk about another group called Centennial Park. These two groups are located close together and many residents are actually neighbors. We'll also talk about black polygamists. Is there such a thing? Check out our conversation.....

The Interview

GT: Let's talk a little bit about the FLDS group. Jumping back in history again. [Did the Musser group] morph into the FLDS Church?

Anne: It was never called the Musser Group. If anything it was the Allred Group that evolved from Joseph Musser. He's the one who called them to a council.[19] He knew it was going to be a separate council from the other one[— so the result was two opposing councils.

Eventually the original council was led by LeRoy Johnson, but they were not identified as FLDS at that time. They didn't call themselves FLDS (Fundamentalist Church of Latter-day Saints) until after 1986. They were just another priesthood council. LeRoy Johnson lived to be 98 years old. When he died, Rulon Jeffs was his successor as head of their Priesthood Council. When Rulon's health began to fail, his son, Warren, started taking over more and more and succeeded Rulon upon his death in 2002.

---

[19] Rulon Allred, Owen Allred, Marvin Allred and a few others were called to be on another council.

In my opinion, at that point things went from bad to worse.]

GT: 1986 is when the FLDS Church really started?

Anne: [It was about then. The Centennial Park people separated from the group in Short Creek in 1984. Short Creek became two communities in 1985: Colorado City, Arizona, and Hildale, Utah, and at that time they had not yet become known as FLDS. The fundamentalists who started the Centennial Park community separated from the other group because they did not go along with the one-man rule that was the predominant policy of Rulon and Warren Jeffs.]

GT: What's the one-man rule?

Anne: [Even though they had a priesthood council, there was one "main guy" who made all the decisions and controlled the members. Everything had to go through that one person. The people in Centennial Park wanted a priesthood council but without such a controlling leader.]

GT: Ok, so let me make sure I understand that. So in the AUB, there's a lot of people that have the sealing power. Are you saying that in the FLDS group, all of those sealings have to go through one man?

Anne: Absolutely.

GT: Ok, so that's one of the big differences.

Anne: Yeah. [There are some on the AUB Priesthood Council, from what I understand, that have been commissioned to perform plural marriages by priesthood authority, but I think such sealings have to be approved by the AUB leader.]

GT: Yeah, so what about in the FLDS group?

Anne: [From what I understand, there is only one person in the FLDS group that has the authority to perform marriages—and that is their leader, currently Warren Jeffs. And he not only performs them, but he appoints who can marry whom, and you were in serious trouble if you refused to marry the designated person.]

GT: These were essentially arranged marriages.

Anne: Yeah.

GT: Like you would think of in India or something.

Anne: [In some cases the couple had enough faith in their FLDS leader, that they went ahead with the marriage against their will and just tried to make the best of it. There is a lot more control over FLDS marriages there than there ever has been in the Allred group.]

So Centennial Park, they now have about 2,000 members, they separated from the other main [group]—they weren't even called FLDS until after Centennial Park separated. So that's why they don't like to say, "oh we separated from the FLDS," because it wasn't even called the FLDS at the time they separated, but technically you get the picture.

GT: Ok, so Centennial Park really was the one that came out and FLDS separated from them?

Anne: [That's what Centennial Park might say, but the FLDS would say the opposite. It depends on who you're talking to. In other words, they separated. The two members of the priesthood council in Short Creek that were asked to leave started the separate council in Centennial Park. Many of them moved to a new community a few miles southwest in Arizona. Most of the

Centennial Park people, however, who had homes in Short Creek stayed there and are there to this day.]

GT: Ok. So I know the FLDS are pretty distinctive with their dress. A lot of them have long-sleeved dresses that go all the way to their ankles. Are Centennial Park styles similar?

Anne: Similar, [but not as extreme. They dress modestly. I think that you can readily tell the difference between the appearances of FLDS women (the ones that follow Warren) and those in Centennial Park. The women among Warren's followers wear distinctive solid color dresses of a certain style. Their hair is pretty much one main style, although there is some variation.

But the ones who have broken away might still wear long sleeves and long dresses. Centennial Park women usually wear long sleeves, and some of them even wear pants. They aren't instructed as to exactly what to wear, but they dress modestly.]

GT: Now I remember there was a story, I'm trying to remember which book that was, several years ago, a funny story about a young man; they were living the Law of Consecration. I think it was *The Great Basin Kingdom*.[20] I might have the book wrong. At any rate, everybody had to wear the same clothes because they were living the Law of Consecration. One young man took some of the leftover wool and had a different pair of pants made. The Law of Consecration, they all said…

Anne interrupts: It's really the United Order, [not consecration.]

GT: United Order, right. Everybody had to wear the same clothes so they all looked the same. It's a really funny story.

---

[20] See http://amzn.to/2iRzYhR

Anne asks: And did he back up against the grist mill to wear out his pants so he didn't have to wear them anymore?

GT chuckles: I don't remember that. So are the FLDS the ones [who have the same style dresses?]

Anne: [Pretty much. They vary in color—most of them being solid lavender, purple, blue or pink.]

GT: Ok, and their hair style—is that because they are trying to live this United Order/Law of Consecration?

Anne: I think Warren (No. 1) wants to exercise power and control over the people; and (No. 2) he's trying to have everybody look equal—except [these styles don't necessarily apply to him. He could wear whatever he wanted.

It's hard to say that this is the way these people always dress, because right now things are in such a state of flux and very confusing.]

GT: Ok, going back to that, it seems like the FLDS and perhaps Centennial Park are very conservative in their views. We were talking a little bit about the gay issue a little earlier. Would you think they would be as open as you are on the gay issue, or would they be against gay marriage?

Anne: I really can't answer for them, but I think there would at least be some that are ok with legal gay marriages as a civil right. They [should] have their civil rights to form a family, just like we [should have] our civil rights to form our families— leaving religion out of it.

GT: Ok, I've also heard regarding the FLDS, and let's include the AUB and Centennial Park as well—[what do they think of the 1978 revelation opening the priesthood to all male members of the church? Is it true that [they] don't recognize that revelation? Do they still believe in the Curse of Cain, Curse of Ham doctrines?

Anne: [To begin with, most fundamentalist Mormons seriously question that the 1978 announcement was really a revelation from God. I can't answer for FLDS or Allreds as a whole. But I think, generally speaking], fundamentalist Mormons do not believe that the time has come for the black race to receive the priesthood, and maybe I just better let it go at that.

GT: Ok.

Anne: Because I don't want to appear bigoted or racist or whatever, but there are many scriptures and early leaders' quotes [that do not support the church's decision regarding the blacks. One of the books Ogden wrote was on blacks and the priesthood, so I'm familiar with the pertinent background and history.] I just question the timing on it.

GT: Ok, are you aware of any polygamist group, because we've talked about three, and I know there's a lot more than three out there, are you aware of any groups that do have black polygamists, or allow black members in their groups?

Anne: I don't.

GT: You don't. So it would seem that those Curse of Cain, Curse of Ham are still well-entrenched in most. Is that a fair statement?

Anne: I guess. It's so controversial and it's hard to explain so other people understand it. I don't see anything wrong with blacks joining the church and having equal civil rights, but [receiving the Priesthood is a separate] issue.

GT: It's a civil rights issue, not another issue. Ok, I won't push that any more. Let's talk about some of the other groups out there. Before we started recording, you and I had a conversation about the FLDS group in particular. One of the things you mentioned was [that their numbers were pretty large and now they have dropped considerably.] Can you tell me what you think the high water mark was for their membership and where it is now?

Anne: [I think it was about 10,000 in the day before all these breakoffs and factions and before Warren Jeffs took over. I arrived at this figure by talking with people connected with the group and also from media who were very familiar with what was going on in that area. When Warren took over and began banishing people, the numbers began to decrease rapidly. There was one Sunday when Warren called the names of 21 men from the pulpit and said, you're out of here. Pack your bags and go. He brutally split up countless families over several years. I've heard so many stories about Warren's atrocities that I wouldn't want to be in that man's shoes because he has caused so much heartache among the families there. Hundreds of them reached their limit as far as following him and they have just left.

What's sad now is that Warren himself is telling the people to leave rather than pay the $100 monthly assessment on their property. He has told them that they are on their own, so they are moving out with very little job training or money and with little more than the clothing on their backs. They are moving to other Utah communities and starting all over. There's one story after another about what's happening to the people who no longer want to follow Warren.

Fortunately, there are some organizations that are helping these desperate people. *Holding out Help* is one of them. They have assisted over 1,500 "refugees" that didn't know what to do once they left. They have provided housing, jobs, financial training, and education. They are an amazing organization.

The *Hope Organization,* with headquarters in St. George, [Utah], is still involved to some degree. *Cherish Families,* sponsored by the Joe Darger family, has been successful in helping many individuals and families who have left various groups.

I have no idea what the population is of Warren's followers or even those that live in the towns of Colorado City and Hildale. I guess you could find out that information by talking to the mayors of Colorado City and Hildale, but things are really in a sad state of affairs.]

GT: Ok, so just ballpark. Do you think it's one-half of what it used to be?

Anne: I couldn't even begin to tell you. I did read an article in the paper [recently where the reporter interviewed one of the former members of Warren Jeffs group, and she said that she thought there were more ex-FLDS members than there were current followers of Warren Jeffs.]

GT: Have they joined with other groups like Centennial Park?

Anne: Oh no, they will not [have anything to do with Centennial Park, unless it's a very rare occasion. Centennial Park members have been there to help FLDS teenagers and have offered to open their homes, if they needed a place to stay, but to followers of Warren, Centennial Park is the enemy because they broke away from their priesthood, in their opinion. They are considered apostates.]

Ervil LeBaron: Polygamist, Assassin

Introduction

We're going to talk more about some of the smaller polygamist groups, such as the Kingston group and Harmston group. We'll also talk about the infamous Ervil LeBaron: a polygamist and an assassin. He was responsible for the deaths of not only his own brother, but other fundamentalist leaders such as the Apostolic United Brethren's Rulon Allred. We'll talk more about this infamous man, who died in a Utah prison in 1981. Check out our conversation.....

The Interview

Anne: [In discussing other groups: There's the Davis County Co-op or Kingston Group. They have about 2,000 members. Their leader is Paul Kingston. He's in the South Salt Lake area. They started in 1935 as a United Order organization, not necessarily a polygamist or religious organization. Today some of their members are polygamists, but not all.

They wanted to find ways of supporting their families on an economic level. The United Order was the thing that got them going. I know several of the people in that community, and the women are amazing. They are hard-working, have large families and many have full-time jobs outside the home.

Some smaller groups: There is one in Manti that pretty much is now down to very few families—the Jim Harmston group. There is *the Branch* (now officially called "Christ's Church") that was started by Gerald Peterson in the late 1970s. His son Gerald Jr. succeeded him upon his death in the early 80's, and he is still the leader of that group of about 200 members.]

GT: It's called *the Branch*?

Anne: [There are other small break-off groups, as well, such as the Nelson/Naylor group that separated from Centennial Park. They have a priesthood council and about 300 members.]

GT: 300! It's a very small group.

Anne: Yes, some of the others are even smaller than that.

GT: Would it be safe to say that the AUB is probably the [largest] group now?

Anne: It is.

GT: It's probably about 7500.

Anne: [It's the largest group that is somewhat unified. They have their problems and issues, too. Some will attend meetings, but question the qualifications and abilities of their leadership. There are some internal divisions and loyalty issues. But then the LDS Church has problems, as well. It's a tough time right now for many religious organizations.

And we can't forget the independents! That's what I am. I consider myself an independent fundamentalist Mormon, and that's because I don't belong to any organized group. There are about 15,000 independents in the western states.]

GT: Oh, so they're the biggest.

Anne: [But we aren't a group. Generally, we believe in keeping these eternal principles alive, not just plural marriage but others as well. We don't feel impressed to join any of the fundamentalist groups.

GT: Ok, so unaffiliated independents are kind of the largest fundamentalist Mormon segment?]

Anne: Yes

GT: So would that include LDS members secretly practicing polygamy? Would you consider them independents as well?

Anne: [Probably. Or it could include fundamentalists that believe in those early doctrines, don't necessarily live plural marriage, but they want to raise their kids in the LDS Church. I know families like that, and so they keep quiet about their beliefs. They attend church meetings and carefully go along with the program. Sometime they may reach a point in their life where they feel like they can't support the mainstream church anymore, so they just become inactive.]

GT: Ok, as well as maybe FLDS who have left or AUB who have left or Centennial Park who have left?

Anne: [I don't know that many former FLDS members have joined the LDS Church, but some of the AUB and independents have become members.]

GT: What I'm saying is there are probably breakoffs from each of these groups that would be independent. That's what I meant to say.

Anne: I guess so. That's going to vary because some of them may not believe in fundamentalism at all anymore. There are some teenagers that were so controlled [when they were younger that when they left their community, they became pretty wild—got into drinking, loose women and other unsavory activities. There are some that don't want a thing to do with religion so you couldn't call them independent fundamentalists.]

GT: No, they would just be non-religious.

Anne: [Yeah, they've gone in their own direction. So like I say it's really confusing when you try to designate or define this group or that group. It's pretty hard to draw definite lines because conditions are kind of hazy.]

{break}

GT: I want to ask you about another group I've heard of: Ervil LeBaron. Can you talk about his group? That's an interesting group.

Anne: Well, [Ervil] came from a family that claimed to get their priesthood through Benjamin F. Johnson. According to the story, Benjamin Johnson was the adopted son of Joseph Smith, and so he passed the priesthood on down through that line. It was a large family. Ervil LeBaron was one of the older sons, and they felt like theirs was the only true lineage of priesthood.

[According to news reports, Ervil was responsible for the deaths of about 20 people. I can verify that because I knew some of them. My husband, Ogden,[21] and I had been introduced to him one time when Ervil was using a fictitious name. At this meeting he was introduced as Mr. Stilson. But shortly afterward we saw a photo with a caption that said: "Wanted: Ervil LeBaron"—but the photograph was of this Mr. Stilson that we had met at this meeting. Ervil had even stayed in my home under that assumed name. When I found out who he really was, I

____

[21] Anne was the second wife of polygamist Ogden Kraut.

was a little concerned; but fortunately I didn't know who he was at the time he stayed in my home.

Ervil and his followers demonstrated a very different aspect of fundamentalism. I have never really considered his being a fundamentalist Mormon. I guess, generally speaking, you could say that. There's a colony in Mexico named Colonia LeBaron[22] that has a lot of peace-loving LeBaron family members, but Ervil's self-appointed mission was definitely more militant: "You either follow me or else." Ogden got a letter from Ervil to that effect, and we were quite fearful for a while about the "or else." I could relate an interesting story about that, but I think I'll pass for now.]

GT: Let's back up a little bit. Where did he claim to get his priesthood authority from?

Anne: [From his father, Alma Dayer LeBaron. He got it from Benjamin Johnson who claimed to be an adopted son of Joseph Smith.]

GT: So from Nauvoo?

Anne: Yes

GT: Ok, that's from 1840, and this is....

Anne: Oh, that didn't come down from the 1886 [revelation] at all.

GT: I'm just wondering because Ervil was a polygamist. Is that correct?

Anne: Yes

---

22 Colonia LeBaron is located in the state of Chihuahua, Mexico.

GT: [Does Ervil LeBaron tie into the Allred (AUB) group, Centennial Park, or FLDS?]

Anne: No, they came through a totally different line.

GT: So he was more of an independent?

Anne: Oh, I don't want to call him an independent. I don't want to claim him. {chuckles} Ervil was responsible for Rulon Allred's death. He sent two of his wives to kill him.

GT: So why did he do that?

Anne: Because he was a very jealous, power hungry guy. [He thought he was the only one who had priesthood authority so everyone was supposed to follow him. He wrote a threatening letter to four people and Ogden's name was one of the four, along with Rulon Allred. When Rulon came up dead, we were very anxious for a while.

He had Rulon killed, and also killed his brother, Joel.[23] His brother, Verlan, started to write a book on the LeBaron family, and when he died unexpectedly in a car "accident," Charlotte, one of his wives, finished it.]

GT: So LeBaron had a bunch of wives that became a bunch of essentially assassins to kill people.

Anne: I don't know if it was always [his wives. Ervil sometimes used some of his loyal followers.]

GT: But some of them were.

Anne: He just sent people to kill other people.

---

[23] Ervil killed his brother Joel in 1972, and was convicted in 1980 of trying to kill another brother. See http://www.nytimes.com/1981/08/17/obituaries/ervil-LeBaron-utah-polygamist-is-found-dead-in-his-prison-cell.html

GT: Because he just basically wanted to consolidate power in the polygamist Mormon community?

Anne: [Ervil firmly believed that he was the one mighty and strong that is spoken of in D & C section 85. He was the one who was supposed to take over everything. There are so many stories connected with this.

GT: So he was his own man. There is a LeBaron group now. Is that true?

Anne: [Yes, I guess you could call it a LeBaron group, consisting mostly of the LeBaron brothers' descendants. There was a lot of jealousy among these LeBaron brothers. Ervil was finally arrested and died in prison.]

GT: Ok, so this is probably in the 1970s when he's killing Rulon Allred and some of these others. Is that right?

Anne: [Yes. Rulon died in 1977 in his Murray doctor's office.[24]

GT: It seems as if Ervil was trying to go after President Kimball. Have you heard that or am I making that up?

Anne: Oh, he had a lot people on his hit list. The church authorities were very concerned. They doubled security for a while because Ervil had made death threats.]

GT: Against lots of people.

Anne: Against whoever was president of the church at the time.

GT: But he's responsible for about 20 deaths.

Anne: That I know of.

---

[24] Rulon Allred died May 10, 1977.

GT: Maybe more. It's kind of a strange story.

Anne: The person in whose home we were in when we first met Ervil—that guy came up missing the next week.

GT: Oh, you're kidding!

Anne: We know only too well what happened to him.

GT: Was his body ever found?

Anne: [I believe it was, but I do remember that the death was definitely pinned on Ervil.]

Anne's Marriage – Was Jesus a Polygamist?

The Interview

GT: Could I ask you about your life with Ogden?

Anne: Sure.

GT: Your husband was Ogden Kraut. Are you from the Salt Lake area, or was that up in Weber County that you were [married]?

Anne: I never lived in Weber County.

GT (chuckles): I guess the name Ogden screwed me up a little bit.[25]

Anne: Oh yeah. [My husband's name was Ogden, but he wasn't from Ogden.

Just quickly–I was born and raised in the LDS Church, very happy in it. I went to BYU on a scholarship, graduated with honors. A year after I graduated, I married (in monogamy) Ted Wilde in the Los Angeles Temple. We were together for nine years and during that time we learned there had been several changes made in the mainstream LDS Church. Ted was very intelligent, a researcher, a scholar, not an author, but knew a lot about the history of the church; so I learned a lot of that from him and also while visiting with many of our friends.

One of those friends was Ogden Kraut. So when our marriage didn't work out, a year after the divorce, I became Ogden's second wife. I was married to him for 33 years and he died in 2002, 15 years ago. We had a really happy marriage, got along very well. He wrote, and I helped him write 65 books on church history and

---

[25] Ogden, Utah, is the largest city in Weber County.

doctrine. It was during that time that we met a lot of fundamentalist Mormons and members of different groups—mainly because of his books.]

GT: Now was Ogden a member of the LDS Church, too?

Anne: Yes, he was later excommunicated in [19]72.

GT: '72.

Anne: I married him in '69.

GT: Ok, so you were both members of the LDS Church when you got married.

Anne: Yes.

GT: I think that most LDS people think that marriage sealings always happen in the temple. I'm assuming that's probably not what happened in your case.

Anne chuckles: [No it's not the place that's important— it's the person who has the authority. A lot of marriages in the early days of the church took place before there was a temple. There are even accounts of these marriages in the Salt Lake Valley. I believe it was John W. Taylor that met a couple at the Farmington train station. He married them on the train going one way, and on the way back they got off and went home. Another couple was married plurally on a buggy ride going around Liberty Park, because this was at a time when things were kind of risky.

There was an endowment house that people were married in here in the valley. They were also married down in Mexico, and there was no temple down there. So it's not the place, it's the authority that seals that marriage. If the person who is sealing the marriage has had

Priesthood properly conferred upon him and preferably has had a calling or a commission to perform marriages, (but that's not essential), his Priesthood authority seals the marriage.]

GT: Ok, so would it be similar to a typical LDS sealing ceremony or is it pretty different?

Anne: No, it's pretty much the same. There is certain wording that should be used.

GT: Right. I would understand that, and I don't want to delve into that too much. So you were both members of the LDS Church. I guess you've always been an independent?

Anne: Right, we never joined a group.

GT: So this was just someone that you felt had the proper authority that sealed you together.

Anne: Right.

GT: Talk about how that was. I would assume that you had to be pretty secretive about that.

Anne: Very. My own parents and family didn't know for quite a while. It's not the way I would like to have had it, but it was essential.

GT: Ok, so you said you had a wonderful marriage for 33 years. I would expect you probably didn't live in the same house.

Anne: [Oh sure we did, but he was not there 24-7. He was in and out. I was his secretary so we got away with going places together because I typed his books. We were good friends, and if anyone asked, Ogden would say, "Well this is my secretary," which was true.

Ogden's first book, *Jesus Was Married*, came out in February of 1969. Joseph F. Smith was president of the Quorum of Twelve at that time, and Ogden knew he believed that Jesus was married. So as soon as the books came out of the bindery, we took the first copy up to Joseph Fielding Smith. His secretary was there, and at that time you could walk right in practically and see a general authority. His office door was open. We asked his secretary if we could we give him this book. She motioned us in. When we gave him the book, Ogden asked, "What do you think?"

He said, "Oh, absolutely he was married. It could be no other way. The account of his marriage is right there in the New Testament (referring to the marriage at Cana)."

With that endorsement, we took the book around to some of the bookstores. We sold the first 500 copies in a very short period of time. That's been Ogden's most popular book. We sold several thousand.]

GT: Jesus Was Married.[26]

Anne: Yes.

GT: Ok, so you're saying that the wedding feast that Jesus turned water to wine, that was Jesus' wedding?

Anne: [Yes, that was His wedding.]

GT: Who did He marry?

Anne: Probably Mary.

GT: Mary Magdalene?

Anne: He had at least three wives.

---

[26] See http://amzn.to/2huwWzS

GT: Three wives?

Anne: Yes. Mary, Martha, and Mary Magdalene that we know of; there's a quote that kings' daughters were among his honorable wives.

GT: Kings' daughters were among His honorable wives?

Anne: … among Christ's honorable wives.

GT: I don't understand what that means: Kings' daughters?

Anne: He married kings' daughters. Kings' daughters were among his honorable wives, meaning the Savior's wives.

GT: Ok, so are you referring to Mary and Martha being the kings' daughters?

Anne: Not necessarily, but Mary Magdalene was from royalty.

GT: Mary Magdalene was from royalty?

Anne: Yeah. [The New Testament translation on that, like we discussed earlier, is incorrect.[27]]

GT: I don't see that in the Joseph Smith Translation[28], or is that from revelation? How do you come up with that?

---

[27] The 8th Article of Faith says, "WE BELIEVE THE BIBLE TO BE THE WORD OF GOD AS FAR AS IT IS TRANSLATED CORRECTLY." A September 2015 Ensign article at LDS.org gives more information. See https://www.lds.org/new-era/2015/09/to-the-point/what-does-the-eighth-article-of-faith-mean-when-it-says-we-believe-the-bible-to-be-the-word-of-god-as-far-as-it-is-translated-correctly?lang=eng

[28] Joseph Smith believed that many errors were in the bible and many plain and precious parts were removed. As early as 1831, he received revelations restoring many lost verses, and these extra verses are known as the Joseph Smith Translation of the Bible. The LDS Bible has various verses added as footnotes, as well as an appendix. The Community of Christ retains the original

Anne: You'd have to read [Ogden's] book. There are a lot of references. Joseph Smith, for example, told two or three people, "You are direct descendants of Jesus Christ." You can't be that unless He had children, which He did.

Christ always said, "Come follow me." Well he didn't say, "Come follow me but don't get married." I mean it's just one thing after another. You just kind of put it all together. A marriage being as important as it is, can you imagine the Son of God not being married?

GT: Hmmm. I don't know. Does the LDS Church have a position on whether Jesus was married?

Anne: Oh they don't like you talking about it. That's another story. When we put this book out, we went down to Provo and E.L. Whitehead was in charge of the Seventies Bookstore in Provo. This is in '69. We took in ten copies of *Jesus Was Married* and said, "Maybe you'd like to put this out in case anybody is interested in that subject."

"Oh gee, I don't know. Well, I'll put it in the back, and if anybody asks for it, then [I'll get it for him."

Well, in two days he had sold them all and he called and said, "Can you bring me 20 more copies?" Come to find out, he had decided to put the books right by the check stand, the cash register. As customers left, they would see that book.

About this time the religion professors at BYU—Rodney Turner, Hyrum Andrus, and others—were being told by

---

copyright, and has these verses added as their official version of the Bible, known as the Inspired Translation. For a basic history, see
https://en.wikipedia.org/wiki/Joseph_Smith_Translation_of_the_Bible

church authorities not to talk to their students about Jesus being married, as the church didn't have a position on it. We were acquainted with both Hyrum Andrus and Rodney Turner, and they just told their students, "Well we can't say anything about it, but there's a book down at Seventies Bookstore. You can go down there and get that."

Because these two professors believed Jesus was married, but they knew they had to obey the church authorities, this was a good solution for them. Our book sold really well at the Seventies Bookstore because the students would buy a copy and spread the word. Anyway that was just kind of an interesting story. The timing on that was just right.]

GT: That's interesting. I have not heard that. So Mary, Martha, and Mary Magdalene [were Christ's wives. So He] had two Mary wives. {chuckles}

Anne: Yes, He did.

GT: Are there any others that you believe?

Anne: Well, I can't give you names, but there were [others. Yeah, it is said that He] had a trail of women.

GT: How many would you say?

Anne: Oh I'm not going to guess. I don't know, but at least three.

GT: Ok, that's interesting. I might have to check out that book. That was published in 1969 when you were both members of the LDS Church.

Anne: [Oh yes, and I was going to add that our book came out in February and we were sealed in September of that year.]

GT: Ok. That was the year you were married. Cool, so Ogden has written a lot of books. What are some of the other important books, I guess with regards to polygamy especially? And also did he write any other books that were not polygamy related?

Anne: Most of them.

- Gift of Tongues,[29]
- Gift of Dreams,[30]
- Seer Stones,[31]
- Calling and Election,[32]
- 6 books on priesthood,[33]
- 3 books on Kingdom of God.[34]

[The Kingdom of God was a separate organization from the LDS Church; Joseph Smith said they were definitely two separate organizations. The Kingdom of God is political, and the church is ecclesiastical. Today we have quotes that church leaders think the Kingdom of God and the church are the same thing. That's not the way it was originally explained.

- Calling and Election,[35]

---

[29] See http://amzn.to/2izjnQC
[30] See http://amzn.to/2j9YiM4
[31] See http://amzn.to/2iAX39f
[32] See http://amzn.to/2hIdKyT
[33] See http://amzn.to/2hG5Bed
[34] See http://amzn.to/2z6LmgY
[35] See http://amzn.to/2hIdKyT

- The Seventies,[36] (and how they decreased in importance)
- 95 Theses,[37]
- Principle or Personalities,[38]
- Compromise and Concession.[39]

Some of these books mention plural marriage, but there are only one or two written entirely on the subject.

- Polygamy and the Bible[40] was the big one.

The Old Testament mentioned plural wives frequently, and there are also ways of understanding that it was lived during New Testament times, as well. For example, a man couldn't be a rabbi without being married. Jesus was a rabbi. There are several evidences like that and quotes from Celsus and other early historians who were contemporaries of Christ.

GT: I think that the rest of the Christian world would find that quite heretical.

Anne: Oh yeah, that's ok.

GT: Have you had any experiences with talking to evangelicals or Catholics or anybody like that?

Anne: Not personally, no.

GT: Ok, that would be very interesting.

Anne: It makes sense to me.

---

[36] See http://amzn.to/2hOVNCu
[37] See http://amzn.to/2z77tDW
[38] See http://amzn.to/2hEUdPB
[39] See http://amzn.to/2z5xVxl
[40] See http://amzn.to/2zlk4rl

Concubines & Law of Sarah

The Interview

GT: Another question I wanted to ask you, let's talk a little bit about D&C 132, the revelation on marriage. This came up in a conversation this past week. There are some women in the LDS Church specifically [who are concerned about] a few verses in there that refer to Emma Smith that say if you don't consent to this polygamy, you are going to be destroyed. Now it seems like Brian and Laura Hales say that D&C 132 didn't go through the same editing process[41] that a lot of the other revelations did. Joseph was killed soon after. What are your feelings about those references to Emma specifically, that she would be destroyed if she didn't consent to polygamy?

Anne: Well you have to understand what is meant by *destroyed*. Does that mean her exaltation? Does it mean something else? It's important, I think, because also in that area [the scripture] talks about the Law of Sarah.

GT: Yes, a lot of women have problems with that, too.

Anne: Yeah, ok. Ideally the Law of Sarah is that the first wife gives consent for any subsequent wives. If she does not give her consent, then it says that the man is exempt from that law, which is the case with Joseph Smith. Emma didn't give her consent except for a couple of instances, so he was exempt from that law. He could go ahead and take wives without her consent according to section 132, and I believe that's the case.

GT: So why have a law if you're exempt from it? Is that really a law?

---

[41] See our discussion with Brian Hales:
https://gospeltangents.com/2017/06/12/polygamy-dc-132-conflict-jst-genesis/

Anne: Well it's an ideal law, if things were [ideal, but without the law of Sarah, the woman would have control over the family, who came in it, who her husband married, etc. Plural marriage is a priesthood law; it is not a matriarchal law. The man is obligated—both Ogden and I believe—to try and be as patient as possible with the first wife and explain the principle] to her, have a period of time where you are working with her if she's opposing it, and then if it comes to a point where you can see that she's never going to accept that, does that mean his exaltation is jeopardized because the first wife won't let him live a celestial law? That doesn't make sense. It's a Priesthood law, not a woman's law.]

[But the husband is supposed to work with his first wife and try and bring her along, but if she doesn't accept it, then he's exempt from that law of Sarah, which means he can go ahead and take a plural wife without her consent.] Of course I believe you can't get to the highest degree of the Celestial Kingdom unless you live celestial plural marriage. I wrote a book on that.

[Joseph Smith's exaltation would have been prevented] had he not been able to take another wife and live plural marriage. Do you see what I mean? I know this is probably not your belief but I very strongly believe that's the case.

GT: I understand that. Most LDS women, I'm going to try my best to channel my LDS woman here, but they're going to say, "Well look. You're telling me—to me the Law of Sarah, if a man can be exempt from the Law of Sarah, what's the point having a "Law of Sarah?" It's more of an idea. It's ideal.

Anne: [No, it's really an ordinance. In fact, during the plural marriage ceremony, the first wife] is supposed to put the hand of the future wife, the prospective wife, into the hand of her husband. That's part of the ceremony. But if she doesn't go along with it and is not going to be there, he's exempt from that. It just makes sense to me.

GT: All right, there's the scripture: "Neither is the man without the woman, nor the woman without the man in the Lord."[42] If they're not in this together, you said, why should the woman stop the man from exaltation, but why should the man stop the woman from that as well?

Anne: She has the opportunity as well. The door is open for her to accept it. He's not going to force her.

GT: Well but he is forcing her if he's taking another wife against her will, right?

Anne: But he's not forcing her to take part in the ceremony. He's not forcing her to give that wife to him, but he still is able in the law of the priesthood to take another wife. It's really important. But I can see why Joseph and other people would have to be exempt from that law if the first wife is absolutely not going to go along with it. She's jeopardizing her own exaltation because she won't get the blessings for living it if she's opposed to it. She might have another wife in the family but if she's adamantly opposed to it and did not give that wife to her husband, she won't get the blessings for it.

GT: Ok, well I know there's a lot of LDS women, in fact I know one who said, "I don't want any part of that."

Anne: That's fine. They don't have to have any part of it. That's why it's not for everybody. I look at it as a great blessing. I thank the Lord all the time that I was

---

42 1 Corinthians 11:11

able to live plural marriage, because I have a strong testimony that that's the eternal marriage covenant.

GT: I remember one more question that I wanted to ask you concerning D&C 132. One of the references in there says something about wives and concubines. My understanding of the Old Testament, and I want to key in on that term concubines there, [as we look at them today, concubines are known more as sex slaves, especially with ISIS[43] in the Middle East. The men] would take women who were conquered in war, try to convert them to Islam, and they are not full wives, and it seems awful for lack of a better word.

Anne: Right, oh yes, I agree.

GT: It seems like these are literally sex slaves. So I have a concern about that in 132. It says in there that God gave Abraham and David wives and concubines. It is my understanding of the Old Testament especially, a lot of these wives that David and Solomon had were arranged marriages with other kingdoms. They were there to build alliances. These were not Jewish women. When we talk about the sealing, I can't imagine how if Abraham is marrying a gentile, and many of these wives certainly would have been gentiles, why? In my modern understanding, if you want to be sealed together forever, you've got to be members of the church or at least worthy members of the priesthood. I wouldn't expect Ogden Kraut to go marry some non-LDS...

Anne interrupts: ... unbeliever.

GT: Unbeliever, that's a better word for it, an unbeliever. Why would God sanction concubines specifically? Is that the same thing as a sex slave as we're thinking of now? I'll just stop there.

---

[43] ISIS stands for Islamic State of Iraq and Syria. This group of fundamentalist Muslims instituted a brutal interpretation of Islam in parts of Iraq and Syria between approximately 2010-2017.

Anne: Well my understanding is that they are "lesser wives." They are not covenant wives. They are probably not eternal-type wives. But I think there are traditions and customs in countries that God allows to happen. They may not be His religious way of doing things, but he allows [people] to adhere to the customs and traditions of the country at the time. I assume it was something like that.

Abraham was building up a kingdom, and for whatever reason, God acknowledged that. It was not a religious thing necessarily. We talk about the difference between civil rights and religious rights; they were civil [unions] probably. I really don't know how to explain that any better.

GT: These concubines would have been for time only essentially?

Anne: Yes, correct. Who knows if some of the other [plural marriages] are going to be only for time, too? You have to [live it worthily for it to be eternal.]

GT: Right.

Anne: You can't be collecting wives and think "Oh boy, I've got it made."

GT: Well it just seems strange to me because it does seem like, especially with David, in Doctrine & Covenants 132 it says that he did not sin in anything except in the case of Uriah's wife. I'm sitting here from a modern LDS perspective and saying well look. David probably married someone from some other kingdom, some other tribe that was not Jewish, had nothing to do with that. So I guess it kind of makes sense in the idea that if you're considering this a time-only sealing and God permitted it—

Anne interrupts: Well, at that time, were there really marriage ceremonies? There weren't. You slept with somebody, [and she automatically became] your wife. There weren't marriage ceremonies [as I understand it.]

GT: Ok, well what about Uriah?

Anne: Well [Bathsheba was his wife because he had apparently slept with her. There no record that they went to a "priest" or somebody to be married. That was the understanding of marriage in those days. This had something to do with why Tamar tricked Judah into sleeping with her.]

GT: So it was as simple as that.

Anne: That's the way I understand it. [In the New Testament there was the marriage celebration at Cana, so maybe by that time they had some kind of ceremony, but in the Old Testament I don't believe they had marriage ceremonies. At least it wasn't the usual thing. They might have had something when royalty got married, but not for just an average Joe Schmow.]

GT: Well a lot of those were arranged marriages.

Anne: Yes, right.

GT: "My son's going to marry you, and you're going to get together." I'm not an Old Testament expert. That's interesting they would just [say], "Ok, you're going to be married." I think they would have had some sort of a ceremony.

Anne: Well, you'd think because we're so accustomed to that.

GT: Yeah, maybe, I'll have to get an Old Testament expert on that.

Anne: [Pretty much, I mean you could certainly talk to an Old Testament expert, I might be wrong in some cases, but I think generally speaking that was the case. A couple was married if they slept together.]

GT: Ok, so as far as the concubines in today's world, does that really apply to our life?

Anne: [Oh, I think concubines are defined differently now. I think they are considered more like a mistress. To me, a concubine would be equivalent to a mistress. Isn't that the way you see it?]

GT: Well, I mean yeah, I guess in the case of the Middle East you could call them mistresses.

 Anne: [I think in the past they were part of a harem. Concubines came and lived in the palace or an] estate or something. Today they don't live with the legal wife. They're off someplace else.

GT: So another question is, with Brian Hales, I interviewed him. I should have asked him this question. I may have to schedule another interview with him. There are, I think he said 11-14 [women who were married to other men and then were sealed to Joseph Smith.] I think most Latter-day Saints would find that a little bit shocking. Brian said he believes these are women that Joseph did not have sexual relations with.

Anne: I agree. That's my understanding, but I have no way of proving it.

GT: So I am wondering, would they be considered concubines or lesser wives?

Anne: [I don't think so because they were probably married by Priesthood authority.]

GT: Ok. So they would be a full wife, not a lesser wife.

Anne: [I think each case would have to be considered individually. There were some whose husbands were not worthy priesthood holders. There were some who were righteous men. I think that maybe Joseph was giving these women the option to choose. On the other side, they could choose which one they wanted to be with for eternity.

My personal opinion is that Joseph Smith made covenants in the pre-existence with certain women, and he may have said, "I will give you that option, that opportunity to live plural marriage in mortality. You can accept or reject it." He never forced anybody to join his family. But maybe these women got married to someone else before Joseph had a chance to offer them that, maybe before he even knew about plural marriage. But he still kept his pre-existence commitment to them. He still said, "I'll offer you that opportunity to live plural marriage. You can accept or reject it." That's my personal opinion. It makes sense in my mind.

To me, the gospel is all about unchangeable doctrines and ordinances. But they have to make sense. I don't like to be a part of some ordinance that I can't understand, so I try to figure it out first by using common sense. Then I pray about it and hopefully get a religious confirmation one way or the other.]

Polygamy & the 2002 Olympics

The Interview

GT: Are there any other things that you want to bring up [concerning] polygamy for our listeners out there?

Anne: Well one thing, you kept mentioning FLDS. The trouble with that [term is that people unfamiliar with the Mormon culture and terminology, maybe even some in the LDS Church, have a tendency to confuse that term with the mainstream LDS Church. FLDS stands for Fundamentalist Church of Latter-day Saints. Well, some people think, "Oh that's the LDS Church, the mainstream church. They're still living polygamy and look what's happening. Oh, it's a terrible thing."

So it's unfortunate that the "Short Creek community" named their church FLDS. Not only is it confused with the mainstream LDS Church, but also with other fundamentalists because we use "fundamentalist Mormon" as our umbrella term. Unfortunately, some people then think all fundamentalists are like the Warren Jeffs group. It can be very confusing—so when I do presentations or talk with people, I try to make the distinction that FLDS is totally different. It refers to only one of the groups—numbering fewer than one-quarter of the estimated 38,000 fundamentalist Mormons. (This figure was arrived at when I did a survey about 15 years ago—so it could be somewhat out of date now.)

So it's important for people to realize this distinction. Fundamentalist Mormons are not all like Warren Jeffs. He is the leader of only one group, and the other groups have their own leaders. They don't exercise the extreme power and control that Warren Jeffs does. The LDS Church certainly wants to make this distinction, and I'm more than glad to help them do so.]

GT: Well great.

Anne: This has been my life. [I have my personal testimony based on several spiritual experiences that have led me to where I am today. I know that Ogden is the man I was to marry and be sealed to. I have never questioned that for a minute. We both received spiritual confirmation before making the decision to marry, and I feel extremely blessed to have such a wonderful, hopefully eternal, companion. We got along very well and had what I consider an ideal marriage.

Naturally, we weren't together as frequently as most monogamous couples, but that was not a problem for us. We worked together a lot on the books, and we had amazing and interesting Gospel visits with hundreds of wonderful people.]

GT: Well cool. How many wives did he have?

Anne: I never answer that question publicly. I always say a few. There are reasons for that. [Some of the extended families of Ogden's other wives do not know about the plural marriage arrangement, so I try to speak carefully about our situation.]

GT: Ok.

Anne: [Another interesting experience we had was when the Olympics came to Salt Lake in 2002. A few of us plural wives had just become public. Three of us plural wives wrote a book called *Voices in Harmony: Contemporary Women Celebrate Plural Marriage*.[44] It had been published in December of 2000. That was our "coming out" so to speak. Up until then I had always been very quiet about my lifestyle. Ogden was frequently interviewed by media as he was recognized as an "authority" on what was going on in the polygamy world. During his interviews at our home, I would just sit off to the side. "Don't talk to me. Don't show my face," because many family members and friends don't know that I'm living the principle.

The three of us authors—Mary Batchelor, Marianne Watson, and myself—had decided in early 2000 that somebody needed to provide a better public representation of how this principle can be lived, and not let the women who were leaving plural families and telling their sad stories be the only public voice of polygamy. Certainly these women have a right to tell their stories— we never questioned that—but these three or four women were becoming the only source of information on contemporary plural marriage.

The three of us felt strongly impressed that we were the ones to present the other side of contemporary plural marriage and determined to write a book with a more positive outlook. So we sent out invitations for plural wives to participate anonymously. We asked them to keep their comments short—one or two pages at the most—and suggested they share their testimonies and experiences that demonstrated how this principle worked for them. We got a hundred amazing, faith promoting responses. When our book came out, it was the first publication in recent years relating positive personal experiences about contemporary plural marriage.

---

[44] See http://amzn.to/2zmZ9nr

It wasn't very long before we got a phone call from the [Utah] attorney general's office—Mark Shurtleff wanted to talk to us. He had never personally talked to plural wives that were <u>happy</u> living the principle!

So we went up to his office and had an hour and a half long visit with him. He asked all kinds of questions, and then said, "I'd like to meet with you regularly." We had opened his eyes to how polygamy could be lived—that it wasn't all bad. We gave him a copy of our book consisting of women's testimonies that the principle of plural marriage was a true principle, but not for everybody. It worked for them. So anyway, long story short, we had several meetings with Mark. We were eventually invited to be on the Attorney General's Safety Net Committee to represent the polygamist community and work with service providers that were involved with polygamists. I feel like we contributed in helping people understand more about our lifestyle.

In 2002 along came the Olympics. To many people living outside the state of Utah, the LDS Church is synonymous with polygamy. So we put together 200 press packets containing information about fundamentalist Mormon polygamy—how it could work for some people and the positive aspects of it and included charts and percentages of various polygamous groups, etc. We stressed the fact that we weren't connected to the mainstream LDS Church, but were living plural marriage separately from them

Well when the media came to Salt Lake City from all over the world, they went down to the press headquarters and here were the packets. They talked to local media, many of them by now knew who we were because over a year had passed since our book had been published. The reporters asked, "Well where are the polygamists? Where are the venues?"

As the contact person, I began receiving numerous phone calls to set up interview appointments. Dozens and dozens of national and international reporters came to my house to talk to the three of us women. It was really humorous to see them come in very skittish, very nervous, wondering how do you interview plural wives?

We decided to set some parameters for their questions: we wouldn't answer any questions about what went on in our bedrooms, names of other wives or family members because we don't want to run the risk of their having a problem with publicity, and the other thing was our relationship to the LDS Church because I was still a member of the church. However, we said we would be glad to talk about our our day to day activities, our religious beliefs and testimonies, etc." We gave them several areas about which they could ask questions.

We could see how relieved they were, because they didn't even know what kind of questions to ask. Many of them gave us hugs as they left because they had such a good visit. We explained why we lived plural marriage and that it originally came from the Old Testament—containing accounts of at least 30 men who lived plural marriage in those days. Jesus Christ never condemned it. We didn't discuss our belief that Christ was married to more than one wife, thinking that would be more information than they needed to know. So we focused on the contemporary aspects of polygamy.

Anyway, I don't know how many dozens of interviews we had from reporters all over the world. It was really an education for them and for us. It was interesting to see what questions they had that we could feel comfortable in answering. That was part of our mission I guess.]

GT: Yeah, I do remember hearing about a new organization. It's called *Principle Voices*. Is that right?

Anne: Yeah, right.

GT: It's kind of a polygamy advocacy group.

Anne: [It started because of our book.]

GT: Ok.

Anne: [Because people were calling us for information, we had to have a name. What do we call ourselves? It was just the three of us, and then another lady joined us for a while. We weren't out soliciting members or anything like that. It was just because we were the contact people and we needed a name by which we could be known. We decided on "Principle Voices."]

GT: As in the principle of polygamy.

Anne: Yeah, it's a pun.

GT: That's why it's called Principle Voices. Ok. Alright, I think I'm out of questions.

Anne: I'm about out of comments. {both chuckle}

GT: Alright, well thank you. I really appreciate you talking with me on Gospel Tangents.

Anne: Ok.

GT: We'll let you go.

Anne: Glad to do it! Thank you!

GT: Thanks, we'll see you.

Epilogue

I'd like to thank Anne Wilde for spending so much time talking with us. I hope you enjoyed the conversation as much as I did. I learned a lot. We'll jump back to our conversation with Greg Prince. We'll talk a little bit about incapacitation of LDS Church leaders. Greg has written an essay about that, and listen to some of the conclusions he came up with.

Greg: If you're just looking at this from a medical standpoint, it's inevitable that incapacitation of an LDS Church president will be both more frequent and longer lasting. In a fast-paced, complex world with a growing church, that may not give you the ideal governance.

See https://wp.me/p8I6gx-lA

Additional Resources:

Here are links to the blog so you can join the conversation, as well as videos of the interview.

099: Polygamy & 2002 Olympics (Wilde)
https://gospeltangents.com/2017/11/21/polygamy-2002-olympics/

098: Law of Sarah/Concubines (Wilde)
https://gospeltangents.com/2017/11/22/anne-justify-concubines-law-sarah/

097: Was Jesus a Polygamist? (Wilde)
https://gospeltangents.com/2017/11/20/annes-marriage-jesus-polygamist/

096: Ervil Lebaron: Polygamist, Assassin (Wilde)
https://gospeltangents.com/2017/11/16/ervil-lebaron-polygamist-assassin/

095: FLDS-Centennial Park Rivalry (Wilde)
https://gospeltangents.com/2017/11/14/flds-centennial-park-rivalry/

092: How to Polygamists Feel about Gay Marriage? (Wilde)
https://gospeltangents.com/2017/11/04/how-do-polygamists-feel-about-gay-marriage/

091: 3rd Manifesto Causes Schism: Apostolic United Brethren (Wilde)
https://gospeltangents.com/2017/10/31/third-manifesto-causes-schism-apostolic-united-brethren/

090: Did Woodruff Marry After the 1890 Manifesto? (Wilde)
https://gospeltangents.com/2017/10/29/woodruff-marry-1890-manifesto/

089: Taylor's 1886 Polygamy Uncanonized Revelation (Wilde)
https://gospeltangents.com/2017/10/25/taylors-1886-polygamy-uncanonized-revelation/

Here are some other conversations about Polygamy.

072: Who's the Daddy (Part 2)? Joseph or Windsor? (Perego)
https://wp.me/p8l6gx-ib

We'd also love to have you visit our Amazon Store http://amzn.to/2xSfbjT or our website to see other books on other Mormon topics. Be sure to check out our blog as well at https://GospelTangents.com to find information about future guests and projects we are working on. We would also like to partner with artists and musicians to produce a documentary on this and other topics. Please email us at GospelTangents@gmail.com if you're interested.

Thank you for your generous support!

www.ingramcontent.com/pod-product-compliance
Lightning Source LLC
Chambersburg PA
CBHW051220250726
48655CB00006B/2505